WHAT WE CARRY

Stories Black Women Never Tell

WHAT WE CARRY

STORIES BLACK WOMEN NEVER TELL

Vicki Alexander
Juanita Tasby
Karma Smart
Jacqueline Knight
Kameka Goodwin
Monique Blodgett

Copyright © 2018

Healthy Black Families, Inc.

Source of cover art:
https://commons.wikimedia.org/wiki/File:Operation_Unified_Response_DVIDS242955.jpg
Background: By Willy1914 - Own work, CC BY-SA 4.0, https://commons.wikimedia.org/w/index.php?curid=52296690

Cover artist: *Monique Rochelle Blodgett*
This image represents the emotion that is carried in the faces and bodies of women of color. The original image was of a woman and her child being documented while in Africa.

ISBN-13: 9781984137357
ISBN-10: 1984137352

First Edition, 2018

Table of Contents

Chapter 5: What I Carry

Discussion Questions
Healthy Black Families, Inc.
What I Carry Notes Pages

Dedication

This fascinating series of short, true stories is dedicated to:

- Women, children, and their families in the Black Infant Health Program in Berkeley

- Women leaders and participants in Sisters Together Empowering Peers (STEP)

- Staff and board of Healthy Black Families, Inc.

- Our families who have endured.

Acknowledgements

We are grateful to all those who helped make this book a reality. The vision was borrowed from the team at Pillars of the Community in San Diego, California. Their book, *Reclaiming Our Stories—Narratives of Identity, Resilience and Empowerment*—showed us that there is genius in ordinary people. The ordinary can do the extraordinary. We thank Roberta Alexander, Professor of English at San Diego Community College, for invaluable guidance in conceptualizing our book and giving us the confidence that we needed to say: "Yes, We Can!"

We thank the participant writers in this series of true stories who have all bared their souls, telling us about extremely difficult and hidden moments in their lives. Each is acknowledged in her own personal statement. A special thanks to Monique Blodgett for the title of the book and for many of the photographs. Thanks to Ayanna Davis and Deborah Hailu for their moral and physical support and participation in the project.

We are grateful to *HOW WOMEN LEAD,* a voluntary group of individual women located throughout California, who helped to finance the project through a $10,000 grant and encouraged us through their moral support.

Above all, we appreciate the loving guidance of our Writer/Inspirational Coach/Publisher, Valerie Haynes Perry. She is steeped in the black-woman experience and has brought us clarity, self-confidence, and the motivation so needed to express ourselves in writing. Not one of us has written, published, or been acknowledged for the struggles herein described. Valerie brought just the right amount of love and inspiration to make all of this happen. For this we are extremely grateful.

Enjoy the roller-coaster read.

Preface

In April of 2016, I was sitting at the dining table of my sister, Roberta. She told me about a project she was working on to help students and political activists in San Diego write their stories. The name of the book is *Reclaiming Our Stories–Narratives of Identity, Resilience, and Empowerment.* Nineteen writers had composed autobiographical narratives about their life experiences and how they had overcome difficult and oppressive circumstances.

I quickly got a copy to read and was mesmerized. Here was a phenomenal tool to share with others in order to describe and teach how racism and injustice penetrate our souls and shape our very lives. Told by regular people (not movie stars, professors, or politicians), here was a tool that could be applied to the experiences of black women having children. As a political activist and an obstetrician-gynecologist, I saw a connection between a black woman's experience of pregnancy and the conditions within which we live–sometimes called "social determinants of health." There was a great need to create a way for ordinary people to tell their extraordinary stories about pregnancy, birth, relationships, and child rearing.

We all can probably understand how a poor birth outcome (infant death, sickness of a child or mother, a premie) could be caused by social conditions such as no job, no home, inadequate food, exposure to violence, and so on. But, it is well known that even if a woman and family have worked hard to overcome all these "barriers," a black woman will have twice the chance of a white woman of experiencing complications, a sick baby, or an infant death. And in California, a black woman has four times the chance of dying while pregnant, at the time of delivery or post-partum.

Over the last 20 years it has been proven beyond a doubt that the gap in birth outcome between white and black can be related to racism (individual, internalized, and system wide). There is a connection between all the forms of racism a black woman encounters on a daily basis and a condition called *toxic stress*. This toxic stress is directly related to poor birth outcomes and later in life, poor outcomes for a child in school and an adult in the work force. Thus the inequity continues to spiral out of control.

This writing project, *What We Carry—Stories Black Women Never Tell*—takes the methodology of telling stories with a purpose and applies it through the eyes of black women. Like *Reclaiming Our Stories—Narratives of Identity, Resilience, and Empowerment*, the book you are about to read will help us all—black, brown, yellow, red, and white—understand that when you identify as black (or are seen as black), and you live in a place that is inundated with different forms of racism, your baby has less of a chance of being born healthy; the mother has more chance of dying in labor; and the child has more of a chance of dropping out of school, being incarcerated, and not being given a chance to thrive in life.

What We Carry is just the beginning. As the six writers in this book can attest, some of our stories, when read aloud to each other, brought out the depth of pain in our very souls. The process of being together in the same space leant itself to spontaneously creating a circle around a sister who was distressed and help her stabilize herself in our presence. We began to understand that together, we were addressing the principles of destiny, humility, conscience, and truth and that we are our sister's keeper.

The paths that helped us reach these principles were many, including curiosity, concern, courage, integrity, leadership and, YES, writing our own stories down to share with others. It has been a cathartic experience.

At the end of *What We Carry*, you will find several blank pages. They are there for you to write your thoughts and stories. To prompt you to write, we have shared the Journal and Discussion Questions as modified and reprinted from *Reclaiming Our Stories*.

ENJOY THE RIDE! EXPERIENCE THE THRILL OF
HONORING YOUR STORY!

Preface written by Vicki Alexander, MD, MPH

Oakland, California

December 17, 2017

Introduction

What We Carry—Stories Black Women Never Tell is the product of six dedicated writers sitting together over a period of as many weeks for two hours at a time. Clearly, they did much more than sit together; they listened deeply and brought forth stories waiting to be told and ultimately shared with you, the attentive reader.

A facilitator was involved—a black woman, like the other writers. She provided five writing prompts that were the catalysts for each chapter in this book:

- Black Hair
- Mother, Daughter, Grandma
- Black People in Books and Films
- That Just Ain't Fair
- What I Carry

At a glance, these topics might seem unremarkable, but the writers featured in *What We Carry—Stories Black Women Never Tell* elevated those simple prompts into their own specific form of art. If you would like to discover how they accomplished this task that soon became a goal, simply turn each page of this book and read with care.

Additionally, *What We Carry—Stories Black Women Never Tell* concludes with the following valuable elements:

- Lessons Learned
- Study Questions
- Info About Healthy Black Families, Inc.
- What I Carry Notes Pages

We encourage you to write about what you carry on the blank pages at the end of this book. Who knows? Perhaps you will join us during one of our upcoming writing series.

Now, are you ready to meet the writers? Through the sheer power of their written words, they stand ready to interact with you.

Chapter 1

Black Hair

Juanita Tasby

I am from Oakland, California, born to a family with roots in Louisiana and Texas. I still live in the same neighborhood with my husband, Mike and two baby girls—Joy and Grace. My stories are about Determination and Courage in the midst of tragedy.

The Big Boom brought my paternal family to California to work and build up West Oakland. My mother came to California with her father as a teen. Eventually, both sides returned home leaving a handful of relatives still in West Oakland. They left behind a hard work ethic as well as entrepreneurial spirit. My early childhood was rich with culture and hope, and mostly Jesus!

As the elders in our clan began to pass, my family suffered. And as a young adult, I witnessed the deterioration and premature death of both parents.

I met my husband more than 20 years ago. Having come from similar backgrounds, we are committed to Holistic Healing. We hope to pass on restorative practices that will help our girls build a fulfilling life.

I AM God's child. He is first in my life! A personal relationship with the Holy Spirit is the Key to Life!

I AM self FULL, which means I value a level of self-care that enables me to build enough inner resources to serve others. I AM my husband's biggest fan!

Antennas

Juanita Tasby

Black hair is love, fun, and stressful. Mothers transmit stress via hair with the pulling and pushing and whispering. Grooming black hair is very intimate; one has to just let go and become completely vulnerable in the chair.

My first child has the exact same texture as mine. Her hair is very thick. It can achieve curl definition with moisture and good products. I now have a tow-haired baby with thin loose waves.

Dad has beautiful long tresses and I hate for anyone to touch his hair.

I have big, thick, glorious hair with a zigzag pattern. For many years, I kept it braided or pressed—I never did wear the loose afro hair. I joined the natural hair movement and gave up my extensions, wigs, and weaves. The funny part about wearing natural hair is the stupid things other black women say! They offer to help you with that situation or they refer to my kinks and coils as "nappy-ass hair." And they ask when am I going to finally comb my daughter's hair whose mane is gorgeous in a very Esperanza Spalding kind of way.

Everyone else loves my curls.

I know this older Jewish woman who happened to greet me the day I had my accidental natural hair debut. I had intricate cornrows but wanted to pin a curly piece on the back. She says to me, "What's wrong with wearing your hair just like that?" Exactly! What is wrong with me? What's wrong with how God made me? That's when I decided to rock my own curls whether it was tuff afro puffs, twisted, or wrapped. I experimented with oils and butters. And I discovered that I was actually pretty cute, natural hair and all.

Karma Smart

I, Karma Smart, am a mother of a beautiful son with high-functioning autism. I teach movement arts to young and old— particularly traditional dances of Brazil, Congo, and West Africa. Most of my life has been dedicated to serving my community.

My relationship with writing has been multifaceted. I really feel I learned how to write while studying cultural anthropology in Hawai'i. But that type of writing was more technical and research based. Around that same time, I wrote about inner struggles I was having being in a country I felt did not want me. And since that time, I've had a journal on and off—writing straight from my deepest emotions—which came in the form of poetry or short journal entries. Being a part of this work is an extension of that type of writing for me. I am so grateful to be a part of it.

Me and My Beautiful Black Hair

Karma Smart

Me, and my beautiful Black hair, sometimes I am in love with my mane of wildness and sometimes I'm not. Sometimes I feel like I am in a battle with a friend that has let me down on certain days. And sometimes I bask in its glory of majestic beauty. The story of my love and not-so love affair with my hair began long ago, going back to the days of playing in the yard in L.A. at the age of eight. I remember imitating and wanting to be just like my hair idol, Ms. Diana Ross. Her hair was everything I wanted my hair to be: BIG, BEAUTIFUL, WILD and FREE! This was in the 80's when Diana started to rock her long 'fro consistently. And my hair was so close to being just like that! When I think back, it was BIG, BEAUTIFUL, WILD and FREE as well. I knew that I had the biggest afro in the neighborhood. It was definitely my crown and glory. And I want to get back to that place of feeling like that again: BIG, BEAUTIFUL, WILD and FREE!

Kinks, coils, an abundance of curls, that is what I have. I've gone full cycle going back to the style I had when I was a young girl. Now, at the age of 41, I have such a different perspective. I don't feel like I have naps, or a nappy head. I have grown to realize how beautiful my hair is, how soft and supple it can be with the right kind of love. I just need to be inspired to care for my hair. Don't get me wrong, I have many challenging days, wondering 'What am I going to do with these naps?' I'll be thinking to myself, frustrated and utterly unhappy, with the way I look. Especially since I have a gray streak forming.

But, when I think back, I was in love with my NATURAL hair as a young child because of how abundant it was, but it proved to be difficult to deal with, and at times the pain was too much. And so, at the age of 10, I got my hair straightened with a chemical relaxer, and it changed how I saw myself. My thick fluffy, abundantly full kinky hair was transformed into flowing straight, smooth and easy to "deal with" hair. I have to say, I did like it. And looking back, if I take a moment to tap into the feelings I had around my hair, being a developing young girl growing into her teens, I can say, I had a hard time loving my natural hair for a while. I wanted to fit in.

And at the age of 10 we moved from Los Angeles to a place that you had to search for Black people. I am serious. Me and my mama would get excited every time we saw another Black person in town. I felt isolated and alone, and different, and the last thing I wanted at that age was to stick out too much. It wasn't because the kids weren't nice to me, they were. I was lucky I was in a town of pretty good people. It was my own internalized judgment of myself that made me feel insecure. I thought for a few years there, that I was more beautiful with straight hair. Luckily, I had one beautiful Black woman in my life, named Irasha, who was like a godmother to me. She walked in beauty with her beautiful long locs, and always was a reminder that natural hair is not only beautiful, but it is also regal, majestic, and powerful. Her locs spoke of her connection to the earth, and when I was 15 through the age of 18, I made a strong connection to the land—hiking, swimming, soaking in its power while sitting in sweat lodges and hot springs. So, at the age of 17 I decided to get my hair braided, starting with long extensions. And at the age of 18 when I moved to Hawai'i on my own, and settled into living on that land, I realized that I could fully let my hair be BIG, BEAUTIFUL, WILD and FREE again. And I took out the extensions and started my locs and have never looked back.

My hair has been an extension of learning to love all of me as a Black woman in this society and feeling and knowing I am beautiful.

Jacqueline Knight

I am a black female, 48, and disabled. I love people and am a hard worker. I love the book we made!

I have plenty of stories to tell--I've just needed someone to listen to them.

Jacqueline Knight

My beautiful black hair is natural whether it is in braids or straight. You can wear it dry, wet, and in many different styles. You can wash it, comb it, blow-dry it, curl it, dye it. Black hair is really hard to handle if you do not know what you are doing. I really did not know what I was doing when I was a child.

When I was a child, I had beautiful, black, long hair. But I cut it and got into trouble for it. I stood in the mirror and said to myself, "This hair is TOO long!" So I picked up some scissors and just chopped it off. It all fell on the floor. I tried to clean it up, but it did not work. It was all over the floor. Hair was all in the carpet. And it has never grown back since.

After I cut my hair, I knew I should not have done it.

Kameka Goodwin

I am a "Berkeley Gurl" to the heart, born and raised in Berkeley, CA. I am a proud mother as well as a blessed grandmother. My interest in my community began at a young age with helping my mother run the family child care we have had for 38 years. Eventually, I took my commitment to fairness for black children to Oakland, CA and have spent over 12 years working as a head teacher at

Grace Children's Academy. During this time I have nurtured a relationship with the Black Infant Health program in Berkeley and this union has resulted in positive life-changing choices for the future.

I dove right into action at the City College of San Francisco, which led to certificates and awards in community health, including the prestigious Certified Community Health Worker certificate. The years that followed were the stepping stones to receiving more self-care training as well as countless opportunities to empower my community members.

After graduating from Berkeley City College, the flood gates opened up and a community warrior was born! I am currently a program coordinator for Healthy Black Families Inc. in Berkeley. In my current position, my team and I are able to provide health parties, educational forums, healing sister circles, healthy shopping/healthy cooking classes and a host of other events to help South Berkeley residents regain their power in the community.

My main goal in life is to be happy and create physical, mental, emotional, and spiritual wellness in black families.

My Black Hair Is

Kameka Goodwin

My black hair is **THICK**, like the indescribable bond between mother and child.

My black hair is **KINKY**, like the animated, complex back streets of our resilient urban communities.

My black hair is **FLOWING**, like the endless thoughts and questions of those who have stopped thriving due to the world's cold, corrupt existence.

My black hair is **COLORFUL,** like the countless gifts that erupt from the talented lives of our beautiful African Americans.

My black hair is **TREND SETTING**, like the young people of the new grass-roots radical movements, who dare to stand up for what is right and never give up until the playing field is leveled.

My black hair has **THE AMAZING AROMA FROM MY ANCESTORS** who delighted in the finest spices and oils that always complimented their ageless beauty.

My black hair is **STRONG**, like the child who rises again and again to overcome the odds that are stacked so very high against her.

My black hair is **FLEXIBLE**, like the personality of that single mother who juggles many hats to be everything for that child she's given life to and to whom she has vowed a life of perseverance until things get better.

My black hair is **EVERYTHING**, like the opportunity to rise to another day and feel the soothing hug of the morning sun, that gently guides you into your destiny for the day.

My black hair is **LOVED BY MY BLACK MAN**. Short or long. Wrapped up or dangling locks of red and gold, my man wants to embrace it as the night falls and wake up to it as a confirmation to the authentic relationship shared.

My Black Hair Is

My black hair is **LOUISIANA,** like the busy Mardi Gras streets, the fields, the strong African roots, the life stories, the victories, the culture, the shortcomings, the entrepreneurs, the ghosts from the past, the dreams of what's ahead, and the living spirits of the present day.

My black hair is **CULTURALLY BLENDED,** like the inner-city village who wholeheartedly raises everyone to shoot for the stars, yet never belittling anyone, but always believing that we all have value and we should leave our mark when we depart.

My black hair is **WISE**, like my mother, my father, my grandmothers, my grandfathers, my aunts, my uncles, my mentors, my teachers, my spiritual leaders.

My black hair is **MY CROWN**, I wear it with pride and prestige as did those loved ones who marveled in greatness as royalty back in the "Mother Land" before being abruptly stripped of it all.

My black hair is **LIKE A SPONGE**, absorbing every element that crosses its path. Never biased, therefore always taking the good elements along with the bad. Yet withstanding it all.

My black hair is **IRRESISTABLE,** like finding a relaxing place and indulging in your guiltiest pleasure until your heart is content and happy.

My black hair **LOVES TO BE LOVED,** like that soul who runs from place to place, fighting battle after battle with self to find that just-right spot where it can plant roots, take off, and be remarkable.

My black hair is **ME,** loved, strong, broken, hopeful, shocked, devastated, angry, hurt, blessed, surrounded by positive energy, ambitious, determined, spiritual, knocked down, progressing, curious, damaged, yet still standing as **ME.**

Monique Blodgett

My name is *Monique Rochelle Blodgett* and I am a 30-year-old mother of an 8 year old girl who believes in expression through the arts. I grew up in Berkeley California with a family who used art as a way to communicate. Since I was little, I have found different ways to share with others how I interpret life. Using drawing, painting, sculpting, sewing, singing, writing, photography and acting; I have created a multitude of opportunities to learn and teach others about the importance of helping yourself grow as well as others. My educational background is with a AA in Humanities and a B.A. in Photography and my passion is in teaching and inspiring others through informative talks. My hobbies include cooking, modifying electronics and all the above that I mentioned. When it comes to my writing, I don't have any fear with what I say because my truth is my truth. No matter where I am at, if something or someone is bothering me, I speak up and write out my truth. I owe it to myself to be honest and I used to think that if something needed to be said that I would have to sugar coat it or tell someone else about it instead of the person. The problem of partial truth is that it can become a habit and I found that I was sacrificing my voice and my truth because of fear of the unknown. I also used to think I needed to be by a window or start at a particular time of the night to write but what I have found that there is nothing that can block me from writing anywhere, under any condition. These poems mean so much to me and to be able to stand up and speak out about these problems that have haunted me for many years, is truly powerful. I wish to continue writing stories and books to inspire my daughter and others to speak up in order to be visible and not invisible.

How dare you

Monique Blodgett

How dare you!

How dare you be yourself,

Take up our space, prance around

in our areas

that make us feel

good

How dare you take over this space

That God created

for us

How dare you think

YOU

Are beautiful enough

For anyone,

With your own texture

How dare you

Think

You can leave our styles

And take our money

We give

You

Elsewhere

Oh …How dare you

THINK

That

Your hair

is strong

And versatile

With multiple ways

To show your

(mmmm…Hair)

as a **crown**

how dare you

think

you are equal to

US

to claim space

and try to live

Authentically.

How dare you think

You….

Can tell your children

That their hair

Is special,

To be fought for

And protected

How dare you

Think

Your hair represents life

And it can hold

Life itself in it

For my eyes are being held hostage

As you pass

So put that mess

In a pony tail

Keep it hidden

Don't let those strands

love one another and unite

because it's too big,

too rough,

too tangled

and too different for us

oh you will see

I don't want you to walk next to me

I'm going to find a way to murder your locks

burn your coils

cut your space

and snatch out your roots

so you will need fake hair

to be

HOW DARE YOU

Oh

How dare you

How dare you

How dare you

(under breath)

(Keep that nappy, wild, dirty, coarse hair tamed)

HOW DARE YOU

walk amongst

us

feeling pride

and no shame

How dare you

Oh how dare you…

Vicki Alexander

Born in Watts, Los Angeles and raised in California, Vicki Alexander, MD, MPH, is the founder and first Executive Director of Healthy Black Families, Inc. in the Bay Area. She also founded the Black Infant Health Program in Berkeley in 2000 and was instrumental to the creation of the Alameda County Coalition to Fight Infant Mortality in 1978 to address Black:White disparity in infant mortality rates. Dr. Vicki's experiences as a single African American mother and grandmother have added greatly to her ability to understand and connect with the community. She attributes her lifelong contributions in the social justice movement to a strong historical family focus on the struggle for peace, justice and equality.

"Dr. Vicki," as her friends and patients have affectionately called her over the years, is committed to health equity and social justice and believes that education must be paired with activism in order to achieve results and social change. Her medical degree and residency in Obstetrics and Gynecology are from the University of California at San Francisco and her Master's in Public Health is from Columbia University in New York. Dr. Vicki has served women and their families at San Francisco General, Harlem Hospital, the Community Family Planning Council (serving all boroughs of New York), and retired from the City of Berkeley Public Health Department in 2006.

Dr. Vicki continues to follow her passion as an activist to eliminate institutionalized racism as the main contributor to health inequity. She has been in the leadership of several social justice organizations including the Rainbow Coalition, Center for Constitutional Rights, Reproductive Rights National Network, Planned Parenthood, City Maternal and Child Health (CityMATCH) and other national organizations.

In 2014, Dr. Vicki proudly served as the Co-Chair of the successful "Yes on Measure D" Campaign for a Soda Tax in Berkeley. She has earned public recognition for the following accomplishments:

- Woman of the Year Award, Berkeley: 2011

- Martin Luther King, Lifetime Achievement Award, Berkeley: 2014

- National Jefferson Award for Community Service: 2015

- Alameda County African American Black History Month Award: 2017

- Woman of the Year Award, State of California: 2017

- Madame CJ Walker Award, 100 Black Women: 2017

- Wheeler Award for Community Service, Berkeley Community Fund: 2017

Dr. Vicki embodies a combination of humility, conscience, curiosity, courage, concern, leadership and integrity in all of her endeavors.

A Story About Confusion: Who Am I?

Vicki Alexander

The very thought of black hair brings chills to my body. I think of all the various styles that I see on the heads of black women and cringe at the amount of money we spend on this symbol of beauty. I look at magazines featuring black women, like *Essence* or *Oprah* and see beautiful black faces obscured by long straightened or artificial hair and I think this is quite an industry. In some cases, I think we are being duped to look white. Sometimes, I think we are duped to look like we are super black, kinkier than the next.

Black Hair – What is it all about? My own hair experiences have gone through a plethora of styles. This short story reveals my thoughts as I look back on the variety in my own hair and how the style related to the historical period it represented. I have been on this earth for 75 years and have gone from frizzy baby hair to kinky hair to tight braids, to an afro, to chemically straightened hair, and now to wavy, thin curls.

Hair from Birth through ninth grade – natural, I was clearly a Negro child with four braids on my head. In some places they just called me little colored girl.

Hair in High School – experimenting, hot comb with oil, smells of burning hair, nauseating. Manual Arts High School's student body came from South Central Los Angeles and was Negro at the time. No one paid any attention to my hair. I was just a Negro girl studying hard to go to college and playing many kinds of sports.

Hair in college – had a reverse put in my hair – chemically straightened in order to try to pass for white as an undergraduate. Here is the story. It was the second year of existence for the University of California at Riverside. Of the 1900 undergraduate students in the school at the time, 4 were students of color and one was black – me. Historically—in 1959 the Civil Rights movement had started to have sit-ins at Woolworth counters – blacks were once not allowed to sit at these counters. I joined the Riverside National Association for the Advancement of Colored People (NAACP) in the small town of Riverside for my sanity and participated in the sit-ins with the community. Meanwhile, on the UCR campus, 5 miles outside of town it was a sea of whiteness. I felt isolated and often humiliated because I had a frizzy natural hairdo. My internalized racism kicked in. I was being humiliated because of my hair and I was Negro. One weekend in the middle of the first semester of school I went home to Los Angeles and I had my hair chemically treated. Wow, my scalp was burning, my head was on fire. I swore that I would get through the agony of being a Negro and of my burning head and would pass for white. I did this to myself to get by in an all-white college. Within two years, my natural had grown back. I cut off the straight part of my hair and became myself again. I decided to bury my head in books and get the best grades possible. But, I still felt inferior and not as smart as the white kids. I moved off campus and found a sympathetic roommate - an Italian girl who had experienced life as part of a family who was in opposition to Mussolini and Hitler. Her family was isolated and had to flee the Nazi regime of Mussolini in Italy. She had experienced serious discrimination of a different kind, and was different from other white students on campus. She was friendly and we got along. I finished college in relative peace.

<u>My Hair through the rest of my life -</u> always hard to comb out. I could completely comb it out only after washing and putting lots of conditioner on it. We called it "grease" at that time. This was from the age of 22 to 50. I thought I did not have time for this. WOW, Black hair. Now, at 75 years, that same hair is thinning out, falling out every time I comb it. I can get a comb through it only after a shower and putting a special conditioner called *Beyond the Zone – Split Mender* on it. I do that daily and finally I have come to peace with my curls.

In comes my granddaughter – multiple styles – the real deal. Real black hair - extensions, sometimes a hot comb, she even tried dreads. Now her favorite is natural hair and she keeps trying different products to keep her hair in a natural state. She loves it and I love it.

Black Hair – a symbol of oppression and a symbol of liberation!

Chapter 2

Mother, Daughter, Grandma

Roll Call/Gracie's Line

Juanita Tasby

Let's talk about intent verses impact…

If they only knew how you impacted my life. My future.
My decisions. My actions. And yes,
my pain and my regrets.

It's all so negative, right?

But Baby, oh baby where is the Joy? She here.

Baby, oh baby, where is my Grace? She's here, too.

But hey. Was it all purposely done?

Was it all purposely given?

Was it actually done on purpose?

Were you being led by the divine?

How will I ever know?

You're gone and not here.

Writing has led me to this place and we are all grateful to be here no matter the pain.

It's all in the plan, led by the divine.

All by design.

Well, oh well.

What will they question when I'm gone?
What will they wonder when I'm gone?
Will I have a script?
Will I have any sense?
Who knows, after all is said and done can we ever hide from our little ones?
Because you are me, and I am she, and we both came from her.
I miss my Granny without knowing why did she hide?

Is hers hidden from us all?

Is hers hidden from me?

What was her story?

Well hers is mine, mine is yours, and we both have what is hers.

Roll call: Grace. Joy. Mommy. Mable. Jackie. Doris. Lucille.

Karma Smart

Where are you, mama? It's your daughter, I need you. This is what the inner child in me would love to say. In my family, the roles of mother and daughter have reversed between my mother and me. One day, when I was just twenty-one, my mother told me, "It's like you're the mother and I am the child." I will never forget that moment, it hit me like a ton of bricks. Out of thin air, it came with no warning. Yet, it was a profound realization that I was grateful for, because I had felt that way for many years before that moment and long after it as well.

How did this come to be? How does a child mother her mother? My story comes from the story of two young 19- and 20-year-olds getting surprised with twins. There was joy and there was pain. She had to struggle with the decision of whether she would keep us, she went against our father's first wish. They didn't know they had twins in the beginning, but finding out they had twins changed his mind. I've reflected on the stories my mother told me about that time. Starting a family at that age was not easy.

For many years, I have been the support my mother has needed. Either caring for her children she had after giving birth to my brother and me, or giving her financial support whenever she asked and I could. In my thirties I gave her a car—it was nothing fancy, it was our old car, meaning my family car. And I was at the point where I could buy another car.

Even though I've been there for my mother, as a mother, there were times when I really needed her. Times that I desperately needed her love.

We will continue that story later. I now want to talk about my grandmother, my mother's mother; for me, she was the best grandmother anyone, or I should say *I*, could ever want. Every time we went to visit her, we (my twin brother and I) were welcomed with the warmest, softest embrace—a bosom of love. And I was always ready to eat because grandmama always had something cookin'. And it was always delicious, a sweet treat made with love along with savory dishes from home— Louisiana, that is.

Grandmama always knew how to show us she cared; I felt her love through her food.

Jacqueline Knight

Well, my mom's name was Marie Knight; she was 54 years old when she passed away. I really didn't get to know my mom. At the time, I was 21; I have a daughter who is 27 years old now.

I never knew my grandma, but all I know is we were born on the same day—June 6th. So every time I make a year, it's my grandma's birthday, too.

I was around 20 years old when I graduated from high school because I was a special-ed student. I could have stayed longer, but I wanted to graduate with my class. I was four- months pregnant with my daughter. I had a hard pregnancy and her birth was complicated. Why? She wasn't ready to come. I had to walk. I had to sit in the tub and take a shower, do squat positions, walk down long hallways, and finally she came out!

When she came out, I said to her with a smile, "You're such a stubborn little girl!" All she did was look up at me and smile.

The Woman Behind the Scenes

Kameka Goodwin

I am a mother, daughter, and a grandmother. I am just one person, but I am all three at the same time. It's 7 o'clock in the morning, the car is packed with lunch boxes, backpacks, and the excited little people in the backseat. The streets are packed just as much. On the way to take the mini humans to school. No fear, super mom and Yah-Yah is here. The drop offs are successful at three different schools. Irritation is trying to kick in, but no one else around is available. Everyone else is at work already. What am I to do?

8:00 in the morning. Running to the store to get that last-minute gallon of milk or loaf of bread for breakfast. The lines are long, filled with other last-minute people, yet your doctor stated that you must eat a healthy breakfast every day. You are wise in years and eating is very important. Your other children are too far away to help you out, no problem, daughter on duty.

Off to pay the bills, the water, the garbage, the PG&E, the rent, cell phone bills, etc. The utilities must remain on for the household to function. Another experience with traffic jams, angry employees who hate their jobs and the burden of negotiating figures to make sure the paycheck meets all needs across the board. No help right now, but the mommy hat is on.

Finally, at work. Trying to rebuild from the ground up. There are many challenges and a lot of loose ends to connect, but this must pan out because the family is counting on you to come through as usual. The ups and downs of the day are slightly tiring, but can't stop now.

School is out and it is time to do the evening shift of pickups and drop offs. First pick up is from the school bus stop. The driver is new and the bus is late. The timeframe is becoming a factor, but it is what it is. Grandmother Yah-Yah is there to receive that wonderful bundle of joy who has no idea what the day has been like for **The Woman Behind the Scenes**. With a glow in her eyes, she must tell Yah-Yah all about the day, and once again super grandmother has been tagged in to give of herself to her family.

The second school pick up requires a walk through the school because the middle schooler cannot stop playing and must be found somewhere in the school. The staff are not too sure of his whereabouts, so super mom is on a mission to find the missing child who is in the gym. A lot is going on, but the mother in me must keep it together. Fussing at him about the importance of being in the right place at the right time will not help right now. Super mom brushes it off.

The day has ended. We are back home preparing for the day to start all over in a few hours. I love my roles that I play in my family and in this society, but I wish I had more time to be the person that seems to get lost every day. This person that I am speaking of, feels like a distant memory. I am just wondering and waiting for the amazing, outgoing, spontaneous person to emerge from within. When will she be able to shine in the light she wants to be in? This has become my new role I will take on, a self-explorer. Despite being lost amongst all the family titles, I am determined to rise. I know that it is possible to be a mother, daughter, grandmother, and the person who was placed in everyone's life to fulfill the task assigned to me from GOD above.

Pass the bottle (legacy)

Monique Blodgett

I am here because of you

You are here because of her

And every woman that came before us

Brought forth life into this world

Whether it was a choice or it was forced

However

It is hard to see

Generation after generation

Carry the same solution

To new painful situations that come our way

For I am sad about the way my grandmother had to cope

The hurt I felt when I saw my mother in a drunken rage

And now I am fighting my own battle with the bottle

And this is not a legacy that I want to see my own child imitate

For we all have carried

The pain of betrayal and disloyalty

When it came to the fathers of our children

Whether it was time away

Or a break in between being married

The reoccurring outcomes

Kept resulting into more children being born

While our hearts were still attached

other mothers had been formed

By the passion, pressure and selfishness

of these controversial male forms

Now this pain

passes through our children

As tears of worry drip down from their eyes

they watch, they worry

Feeling something is not right

As our energy sways back and forth

morning, noon and night

Our children wonder

What is wrong with mommy and why is she acting this
way?

Did I do something wrong?

I don't know what I did

is she not happy with me today?

Yet as I stare back at my child

My wordless expression tells its own story

I've seen the pain, hurt, sorrow, addiction, and anger,

Come from those before me

I feel my own regret, shame, tears and bloodshed

That came with defending territory

I've heard violent words in a mental war

and hearts shattering at the moment of the whole story

Yet as I open my mouth and speak my truth

I will tell her

You are absolutely amazing

You are blessed and beautiful and you did not do anything
to me

You are loved and you did not hurt me

Know that you do not need spirits to help you deal with all
your problems

You need precious water to live and grow

You need people who will love you and help you solve them

And even though I have fought for you

Built that brick wall up for protection

We are all just delicate flowers that really want to live

To be watered, pruned, and picked for the goal of real affection

So one day I hope to see this beautiful light of trust

And start to pass the bottle of life to you

And heal with the intentions to love, forgive and grow

As we change generation to generation.

Vicki Alexander

I remember Mom as quiet. She was not a talker. She was a
doer!!! She worked. She put the food on the table. She
kept the kids in line while Daddy was out organizing for
the rights of poor people. He advocated for people to get
social security and earn a minimum wage at a time when
people had neither. He helped organize farm workers in
the Central Valley of California, many of whom were
Black as well as packing house workers in the Midwest.
And in addition he organized against police brutality and
unfair evictions in the black community in Oakland,
California. He was also a member of the Communist Party

My mother and father were both in the Communist Party.
They became members because they believed it was the
best organization at that time to fight for the rights of
Blacks and other oppressed groups in this country. My
mom typed memos, took care of the office, etc., while
Daddy was organizing. He was often gone.

Then came the late 40's and early 1950's and Agents from the Federal Bureau of Investigation were arresting Communists at the drop of a hat. My father was not in our lives for many years. My strong mom and our extended family took care of us kids.

But wait, I got ahead of myself. This story starts back in the year 1942. It was World War II. The US was at war with Germany and Japan. We lived in Watts, Los Angeles, California at the time. My mom went into labor on February 25, 1942. The siren alarm went off in Los Angeles as a signal that the Japanese Air Force was on its way to bomb Los Angeles. The order was given to turn off all the lights in the city and a curfew was put into effect for night time.

When my mom reached the hospital, it was dark. My father volunteered to hold a flashlight for the doctor on duty for all the different women who were delivering. At the time, Watts was half white and half Negro. Fortunately, my mom had a fast labor because many of the white women complained that a black man, my father, was holding the flashlight for the doctor to see what they were doing as they delivered the baby. They asked the black man to leave the delivery room – OVERT RACISM!! My father did not want a race riot to start in the delivery room. So, he swallowed his anger and left the room. Fortunately, when it was my mother's turn to deliver, there was a flashlight held by my Dad where I was delivered and everything proceeded safely. My Mom was lucky because at least my Dad was there when I was born, but not there when my sister was born because he was out organizing.

But, they had no name for me. In 1942 the practice was to keep women in the hospital for five days for a normal delivery. On the day after my birth, the lights came back on – I still had no name. But, the hospital workers and patients and visitors were all yelling, VICTORY. My father looked at my mother and said, "Let's name her Vicki for Victory!" Corny, but true. My name, Vicki, is not short for Victoria, it stands for victory.

FAST FORWARD TO 1984 AND ME AS A MOTHER. I was now 42 years old and unable to get pregnant. I did all the right things. I kept a temperature chart for six months and when I ovulated the temperature went up a tad as it was supposed to do, indicating ovulation. My husband had his sperm checked and the sperm count was really good and the sperm had excellent mobility. The next step (in 1984) was to do a laparoscopy and look at the ovaries. That is where the doctor inserts a tube into a woman's belly through an incision just below the belly button, puts in a long tube telescope and fills the belly with air and then looks at the ovaries, tubes and uterus. I knew exactly what they would do because I happen to be an obstetrician-gynecologist. I knew the complications at the time and I said no. I did not want any more things done to me. I would be very happy adopting. I did not think I needed to go through the pregnancy and birthing process. So we initiated the adoption process.

This was a time of great tension in the relationship between my husband and me. I think it is related to the content of Chapter 3, so I will not tell that story here. But, we seemed to become more and more distant from one another. Just like my dad, my husband was not around a lot of the time. He had been hired at a job that was meaningful and important for his ultimate contribution to the movement and working-class struggle. He was gone a lot as a union organizer – and a damn good one! I did not question the distance I was feeling. Instead, I forged ahead on the adoption path. The first child we adopted was the son of a teen-age mother. After three months, she decided she wanted her child back. This was hard for me. We had brought the child home. He was a preemie weighing only 5 pounds. He was jaundiced and needed attention. He did not want to eat, so lost weight over the first two weeks. I took off three months from work to pay attention to him. I fed him every two hours, slept in the same room with him to monitor his heart rate and breathing. He began to gain weight and responding more actively to stimuli. Then, the birth mother decided that she wanted her boy back. WOW. But, it was something I knew could happen and she had the right to do this. IT HURT!

After six months, we were given "priority" by the adoption agency. Then very quickly I got a call from the adoption agency indicating a woman had just given birth to a child of the same ethnicity that I was. She was African American (no longer were we called Negro or Colored) mixed with Irish and Native American. I went the next day to pick her up from the hospital. Though she was birthed by another woman (whom I would meet later in life), I immediately bonded with my adopted princess. We named her Maya, after the Mayan Indians and Maya Angelou.

The daughter is now 31 years old and a gifted artist, graduated from Cal State at Hayward in Sociology and writes beautifully. She has two daughters and is raising them almost by herself!!! Men are in and out of both of our lives. We are now a foursome: Yanni (me) the grandmother, Maya the mother and my daughter, Samaiah, 12-year old granddaughter and Layla, 4-year old granddaughter. A family of women and girls is born.

Mother, Daughter and Granddaughters, Who Are We?

- We are Strong

- We are Solid

- We are Sensitive

- We are Caring

- We are Devoted

- We are the Change we want to see

Chapter 3

Black People in Books and Films

Walking in the Warmth: Reflections on Warmth of Other Suns *by Isabel Wilkerson*

Karma Smart

I must share this moving moment that I had when reading Isabel Wilkerson's book, *Warmth of Other Suns*. She describes that due to slavery and Jim Crow Laws Black people of my generation have ten times less wealth than our white counterparts; and how the whole system they created made them wealthy; and how that wealth they accumulated generation after generation was passed down. When reading this—taking it in how she amazingly breaks it down—I began to feel the heat of anger rise up inside of me and reignite a fire that had been tamed by the demands of my life. What she broke down in cold hard facts was something I had always spoken about but had never done the research to back it up. And there it was, in detail. I always would say that this country is as wealthy as it is because of the 400 years of FREE labor and raw materials that our ancestors produced to ignite and fuel the industrial revolution of the white man.

This book was liberating to read because it clearly points out how DEPENDANT white people are on us, yet they reap all of the benefits of our labor, and then want to cry afoul when they aren't getting some of ours. They don't realize that they don't own us anymore, never did, and never will.

You don't own my body, mind, spirit, or soul and the jewels that they produce. Those are for me to keep and share with the ones I LOVE.

Why I Like The Color Purple

Jacqueline Knight

My favorite black film is *The Color Purple*. It really took to me when the children were outside playing patty-cake and the father was treating them like slaves.

My best part in the movie is, "I'm married, now!" And also when Harpo hit on a woman; how they lived in the country compared to living in the city.

My favorite character is Whoopie Goldberg (Celie). I love that movie. It made me cry. They need to make more movies like that. I can watch it over and over and over again.

We have a lot of racism in our country. Black people at one side of the table and white people at the other side of the table instead of sitting together.

Kameka Goodwin

I just don't get!!! It happens every time. It seems to be a part of the norm. Every time a disaster hits, the media makes it a point to show my black people stealing from their community. We aren't only stealing, we are vandalizing. I love my people, but why do we have to be in the mix of everything. WHY can't we wake up and realize we are hurting ourselves along with the unfairness of this country?

We are killing each other and killing more and more dreams of us being great. We must do better. We must learn how to survive without going the "easy" route. There are phenomenal leaders amongst us, but we must give each other a chance. We must step out of the house every day and plan on being the best.

My calling will lead to better days for my village and we will shine for all my black people to see and follow. I do not want to see another black person caught on camera destroying their neighborhood for a quick penny. When we have a need, we must rally around each other and address the need.

I believe in us and I know that where there is a will, there is a legal way. The way might not be visible alone with one set of eyes, but if we connect with each other, we can help each other get where we need to be in this world.

I believe in the village saying, "teach one, reach one." If all my sisters and brothers can commit to each other, we will elevate.

Why Mommy Why?

(Dialogue: A mother and her 7-year-old child)

Monique Blodgett

Mommy why is it that black people never play

Any interesting roles in movies like other people?

Why are the people with darker skin always bad in movies
and play the evil ones?

Why can't people that look like me be a super hero

or a fun and happy character?

Why do the little black girls always have attitudes on TV
shows?

Why do the black guys play the cool guy who always
chases girls around?

Why can't a black person play an interesting role like
"Alice in Wonderland"?

Will we ever get to play in good movies?

Mom, why do black people look like they're mad so
much?

Why aren't their more clips of babies with my skin color

being silly and not getting in trouble like the other kids?

Mother:

I hear you loud and clear

I feel your frustration

I see your eyes getting bigger and bigger

As you ask about these things

And I am proud of your growth but ashamed of the truth

At this time I don't know if you are ready to

hear what I **really** want to say to you

but I can help you to ease your mind and breath

I cannot change the way other people act on TV

I can only tell you to turn to another channel or turn the TV off

Suggest a book to you and read to you

Hoping you would back off

But in the times we are in

Everything is handed to your kind

Nothing is filtered anymore

and in the entertainment world

"WE" are either missing or being pushed out on purpose

with an agenda

that shifts the way you see yourself in others

So when you do get older

Just know you can change the things you see

By working to make something better

Or staying away from the social tricks that they stream

Become that positive person that people

Want to watch

Make up your own role model

And help to change other girls' thoughts

But if this is not enough

of an answer for you now

Just remember when you get of age

Mommy will give you the key and

Let you find it all out

So stay sweet

Don't fall prey to the way they portray us

Don't believe that this is the only way to be

Don't see yourself as only something that was made for TV

You are more to the world than a movie

You are precious in God's eyes

And one day if we pray enough

And continue to seek out change

Then maybe we will see better

Role models and action heroes that share many colors

All over TV that will shine

So what do you think about that?

Daughter:

I'll just watch babies smile and play and watch animals do silly things.

Mommy:

I know honey, if that is what makes you happy, then I'll do anything to make sure you stay that way.

Vicki Alexander

How can I start this chapter? HMM! This is real! This is serious! This is REAL SERIOUS!!

My granddaughter, just 12 years old, introduced me to a book entitled, *God Don't Like Ugly*". For some reason, she had chosen it off of the library shelf at the office of Healthy Black Families, Inc. She was so engrossed in reading it that she finished the whole book in 2 days over the summer break of 2017. The day she finished it I asked her, "Did you like it? Should I read it?" Her answer was, "Yes, Yanni. You should read it so we can talk about it." She was serious but hesitant. I was challenged. She had returned the book to the library at Healthy Black Families and I immediately checked it out and took it home to read. I, too, finished it quickly.

Just thinking of the book brings tears to my eyes. The story is about love, hate, life, religion and death in the life of a young girl who grows to be a young woman through many struggles and challenges. It is fiction. It is about child molestation and rape in the Black community at a time when we were called Negroes. It was written by a Black woman and set in the time period of my youth. The music, cultural expression and experience of the Negro church resonated deeply with me. It was just after the great migration to the North and during the years of the Great Depression.

God Don't Like Ugly led me to ask myself, "Is the fact that I have never enjoyed sex as an adult related to having been molested at 4 years of age and then raped at the age of 18? Yes, finally it is clear to me." And, I need to write about these experiences. I need to let it out.

I am so thankful to the *Telling Our Story* project sponsored by Healthy Black Families for providing the space to freely tell this horrific tale. Here, in this safe space I am publicly telling this story for the first time. It is cathartic.

I met the love of my life in 1979. He actually *was* "tall, dark and very handsome." He had dedicated his life to the struggle against racism, served time in prison, took some college classes while in prison and applied this knowledge as a part of the political struggles of the 60's and 70's. He also had two beautiful children by two different women. We were publicly married in the private space of our home amongst about 100 friends from the Bay Area. We were very happy, I thought.

At the time, I had just finished a residency in Obstetrics and Gynecology at the University of California at San Francisco and was working as a doctor at San Francisco General Hospital. I loved working with women who were pregnant, especially teenagers. I was down to earth, friendly and easy to talk to, so they confided many confidential feelings and stories. I remember being jealous because I did not have anybody I could tell about the most horrible experience I had growing up – being molested by a 14-year old adolescent when I was four years old. I also had no one to talk to about being raped by a co-worker the summer after I graduated from high school. These two experiences traumatized me. I was so shocked that I could not tell anybody. I internalized that the act of sex was dirty, nasty, awkward and hard. I repressed these feelings and did not even talk to my husband about them. I did not want to lose him by showing any weaknesses.

The love of my life must have known I did not like having sex and that I just went through the motions. I loved holding hands and walking together. I loved being seen places with him. I loved his intelligence. I loved cuddling. But, the act of sex was difficult. Now, looking back, this may have been due to the repressed anxiety caused by my childhood experiences. I never sought counseling services for this reason. Is this why my husband sought out other women? Even women that I knew? One close friend actually told me he had made advances to her. Sad. Was it my fault because I could not satisfy him in bed. It makes me so sad – that is why now many years later I need to share my story. It is too late to rectify the problem, but, at least I can be calmer in knowing where the resistance to the act of sex came from.

My husband and I were very politically active in several organizations and at one point we were asked to move to New York to continue organizing. We kept ourselves very busy and became the leadership in most organizations we were in. Between the political work and the job of delivering babies, I was often gone from the house all night as many as three nights a week, including weekends. When I was home, I was tired and did not give attention to the relationship.

My husband was also very busy in the union movement and often at long meetings. When I look back, we were becoming estranged.

Fast forward a couple of years. I was in my forties and realized that I did want to have children of my own. However, I had not become pregnant. I had not used contraception. I underwent a few tests for infertility, but felt it would be better to adopt. Though my husband did not feel the same way, he understood and agreed to adopt. I did not know that at this point he was already in a relationship with another woman. Less than one year after we had adopted our daughter, I filed for divorce.

Not all endings are happy, but I had a beautiful little daughter, a good job and was making significant political contributions for change in this world. So, I turned all my attention to my daughter, my work and political activity.

Chapter 4

That Just Ain't Fair

I'm Always There for Them

Jacqueline Knight

I take on a great responsibility for others—feeling, thinking, wondering what a person's doing, what a person's feeling. People always come to me for advice and it ain't fair when I need someone to talk to and no one's there for me. I'm always there for them.

Being a mom, life in itself isn't fair. I grew up in a foster home and life was hard but we had to be here.

God has created us. We are born, we live the best way we can, and we die. We're gonna die one day.

As a person, it is hard. You have to do everything yourself. It's not like being a child and parents do things for you.

Living and breathing are a must. Walking, talking. Did anyone teach us this? Our parents.

Once our parents are gone, we are on our own. And when we are on our own, we have to think for ourselves. We have to make decisions.

Life is what you make it. We do have choices. As adults we have to make decisions to do what's right.

My child's father was not in my life.

Will It Ever Be Fair?

Kameka Goodwin

It's not Fair! How could they just come to his home, wake him up out of his sleep, shoot him, and leave him for dead?

It's not fair that his smile won't greet his family in the mornings when they come by as well as at the end of the day when his bright smile puts all the stress from the day to the side.

It's not fair that he won't see his family grow into their greatness and make him proud.

It's not fair that sleep is a thing of the past since they took a piece of the family away.

It's not fair that getting out of bed and having a productive day is extremely hard to do.

It's not fair that everyone's health is declining as a result of attempting to deal with the trauma of the loss.

It's not fair that reality seems so gray and pointless.

It's not fair that everything is crumbling around her as she sits back every single day thinking of the memories of the good ole days.

It's not fair that she will never know what type of father he will be, nor will she have a little person to continue his legacy.

It's not fair that life goes on, but theirs has stopped and seems like it will not get back up and running.

It's not fair that his family is in so much pain. The grief flows from the eldest all the way down to the ones who are not even in school yet.

It's not fair that the city they love and grew up in is now the center of so much of their stress and anxiety.

It's not fair that they don't feel safe and they want to carry a weapon.

It's not fair that the perpetrators are free living life and breathing fresh air as if they did nothing wrong.

It's not fair that his family and friends will NEVER BE THE SAME. IT SICKENS ME!

IT'S NOT FAIR, AND IT WILL NEVER BE FAIR AS FAR AS THEY ARE CONCERNED.

Monique Blodgett

I heard you have to be twice as good as the others to get half of what they get

But…

If I don't work at all, does that equal death?

If I work worse than them, does that equal enslavement with no pay?

If I work as good as them, does that equal a quarter of what they get?

If I work twice as good as them, does that equal half of what they get?

If I work three times as good as them, does that equal $3/4^{th}$s of what they get?

If I work four times as good as them, does that equal the same amount that they get?

But if I work five times as good as them, does that equal a little bit more than what they get?

And if I work 6 times as good as them, then does that equal double of what they get?

So if I keep working harder and harder and harder and become smarter, wiser and stronger,

Then…

Will I get my right to be human again?

Will I be praised as a beautiful black woman?

Will I now get to celebrate my cultural pride?

Will I get to make mistakes and not be criminalized?

Will I get to own multiple plots of land?

Will I be able to purchase my own island or claim my own planet?

Will I be able to have as many children as I want without judgment?

Will I be able to police my own area without outside forces determining how long I live?

Will I get to travel all over and not feel like the enemy?

Will I get to be president or the president of a corporate company?

Will I be able to invest in clean water and control what is given to me?

Will I get access to clean air and healthy food and get rid of the poison that is bred artificially?

Will I get to do everything that others can possibly do?

Will I get to have my wealth passed down from generation to generation?

Oh, will I get to bring home a check that exceeds my expectations?

Will I be able to access real medicine to heal and not numb the complications?

Will I be able to wake up every day feeling nothing but inspiration?

Will I be able to dress freely without degrading my Godly creation?

Will I be able to speak my mind without being silenced, ignored and feeling frustration?

Oh what will it take for me to be seen equally?

Do I have to become the queen of every **GOT DAMN THING?**

Just so you know that I am a beautiful human being

Who deserves to have everything just as you receive

What? Do I have to create an alternative source of energy?

Do I have to find a cure for every disease that man has made so awfully?

Do I have to travel outside of the earth and find new life?

Do I have to talk to God and bring back a note saying that I was purposely made and qualified?

I mean what is it that I have to do to show you all that I am just as important as you

Maybe so important that I need to govern over you.

So what you're saying is that if I work harder, then I will get something, I guess

But now I realize that the more I work and the more I perfect

The more you still say that isn't good enough and the abundance of pay and perks

I will never get

For you see I believe now that this is all about capitalism and favoritism

Making me believe that I have to work so hard just so you can kick back and

Take in the benefits of my dreams and wisdom

You knew that if you said nothing was good enough that we would have to work and work and work and work

And you would be able to live in success and control the goods of this earth

While I ached over and over and over

and cried over and over and over

oh why is my life so heavy and horrible

As I carry a million jobs on my shoulders

I wonder

If I will ever see freedom for Mother Earth and Me

But still I hurt

From this verse

No

this curse

Out of the law book

To turn

Others into kings and queens

While forcing others into modern day slavery

Telling others they don't deserve

No they are not human beings

But need to do super human things

To gain

A perk

A pity perk

A pat on the back

Because no matter how this black woman works

It is not good enough for you

but let me tell you a secret

I know now that

"Working twice as hard pushes us to put ourselves in a

situation where we can make things easier for the people

that come after us[1]"

and that is a true definition of black excellency

no matter if society does not see

how valuable we are through eternity

---

[1] http://www.lsunow.com/daily/opinion-black-women-face-unfair-obstacles/article_a1a9ec66-9407-11e7-bcd3-fbcf5c5c2530.html

Vicki Alexander

My life has been a series of "IT JUST AIN'T FAIRS."

I never birthed a baby myself – That just ain't fair!!

As a teenager I was a member of the National Conference of Christians and Jews (NCCJ). I went to the summer camp sponsored by NCCJ – called Anytown USA and then Brotherhood, USA.

I was elected Mayor of the town of Anytown, U.S.A. by its residents, the students (campers) who were in grades 9-12. We learned the principles of democracy and importance of leadership. Then the NCCJ kicked me out of the position of Mayor. This happened when the adult leadership discovered I was from a Communist Party family. They did not even consult the kids who had voted for me. Overnight it had become a dictatorship. The opposite of what the camp was all about.

I had no chance to appeal the "Expulsion" decision. A story ran in the Daily People's World. The national paper of the Communist Party.

That just ain't fair!!!

Fresh out of college I applied for Medical School. I applied to several actually, some historically black colleges (HBC), some state schools and other private schools. I was turned down everywhere. Was it because I was a Negro? Was it because I was Jewish? Was it because of Native American ties? Was it because I was a woman? Was it because my family was in the C.P.?

That just ain't fair!!!

I went back into a cocoon. I was mad at the world. I could not understand the rejection. I could not explain all the anger. I participated in sit-ins, boycotts, marches, demonstrations. Then the Civil Rights Act passed and the opportunity to go to Medical School occurred with the passage of Affirmative Action laws in various states, California being one of the first. In 1969 they opened doors to many applicants of color and offered scholarships.

I applied and was accepted at University of California at San Francisco with almost a full four year scholarship. What a difference. I give credit to the Civil Rights Movement that I am now a physician. By the time I finished Medical School and Residency Training in Obstetrics and Gynecology, I was no longer classified a Negro, I was now African American. That seemed exciting.

But, conditions of life for African Americans did not improve significantly. Even with more doctors of conscience and of color. African Americans still died younger and African American babies were sicker and died too early in life. The statistics were and still are appalling.

That just ain't fair!!!

I moved to New York – it was like jumping from the fire into the frying pan. Heroin use was rampant in New York's African American community. It was being dumped into Harlem. A new cheaper and more devastating drug was invented, crack, and was dumped into Harlem in the 1970's and 1980's. The AIDS epidemic was beginning. In New York it was in the Gay and the African American Communities.

That just ain't fair!!

What motivates this racial inequality and racial inequity? Why? What motivates and maintains this inequality based on the color of a person's skin?

- A society

- A world

- Where greed rules

- Where discrimination is accepted

- Where whole groups of people are eliminated

- Where the social category (label) of race is conveniently created

- Where whole races of people are discriminated against

- Where one race is pitted against another

- Where capital rules without consequences

- Where "democracy" does not exist

That just ain't fair!!!

Chapter 5

What I Carry

What Do I Carry?

Juanita Tasby

Do this! Do that! Where is my brush? Have you seen the keys?
Mommy, may I have some milk?

Yes, from valet to night nurse, I do it all, yet it feels like it's never enough.

While completing one task, the mind wanders over to the next.

I've always felt this way. Brilliant as some profess, I only see flaws.
Underpaid worker.

Unfinished degree.

Late-in-life Mommy.
Married but feeling like a Single Mother.

This is what I carry.

Feeling like I'm living life half assed. Rarely feeling like a winner. I would have to guess it came from early childhood. Mommy never applauded me. She took issue with direct praise. Perhaps she believed in something called indirect praise. I could never begin to explain. However, she would sit every night, on the phone, with a Benson Hedges in one hand and her Crown N Coke in the other. Her reports were so awesome and I'd wonder, *Who is she speaking of?*

Memories of Daddy are fading. However, one night he caught me on the phone while I was on restriction. When I hung up and slowly returned the phone to its place, he appeared from the shadows. I'll never forget his declaration:

"See…me and you won't ever be right!"

Oh, the pain through my heart has never really healed.

What do I carry?

I carry the idea that a child should be seen and not heard.

I carry a miseducation about a woman's worth.

I carry a lot that my girls will not.

At the end of my life, I would want my dear ones to carry only the sweetest memories of their Mama. I want them to know that we're meant to be here—loved and adored and cared for.

I care for them in such a way that these girls will have a big and full life.

I want their story to be theirs, not mine.

This intention started with their names. Joy and Grace. The desires of their parents' hearts.

Joy was born during a time of great sorrow.

Grace was born during a time I felt imperfect and unworthy.

I handle these two with care. I can never be too kind, too loving, nor too sweet to them.

I am willing to expend all my inner resources to serve them. To build them. To completely love and cherish them.

And finally I carry my name, "God's gracious gift."

I was named because in their eyes, for that moment in time, they were happy that I was here.

I carry the choice to be that gift.

I choose how life affects me.

I am here.

My journey is precious.

My life is sacred.

I care for myself like a priceless work of art.

I love me, if no one else does.

I will be that gift.

Karma Smart

The power of pregnancy emanated from me. And I was in love with being pregnant. The fullness of life was inside of me with so much love. I had wanted this for so long and was so happy. I was ready to bring this new life into this world. I was glowing. I was also a little comical when it came to being pregnant with my son. I was getting big and I thought, "Why don't I try to get some pregnancy discounts?" Not only that, I had THREE baby showers—that's right THREE; two at two different work places and one with friends and family.

And when it came time to give birth, I was ready. I felt at peace, I labored at home for three hours, talked to my midwife on the phone, went to Alta Bates, and gave birth an hour later. It was truly a blessing being surrounded by the love of family and friends to witness the birth.

Then comes the first-week check-up. Bhakti had gone from 8.5 pounds to 11 pounds in one week! "What have you been feeding him?" the pediatrician asked in amazement. "Do you have steroids in your milk?" she jokingly asked.

Then the second well-baby check-up came around, and the energy was very different. It was time for the vaccines; I wasn't prepared for all of the fear tactics that were dished out by this pediatrician. Ironically enough, she had a baby of her own in the room that was just a few months old sitting quietly in car seat somewhat lifelessly, as my son's father pointed out. Was it because of all of the vaccines the doctor had given her child? The ones I had just refused to give my own child?

I feel grateful that we had the freedom to choose based on our beliefs, and I believe that is how it should be. Every parent has to make challenging choices every day. At the end of the day, we have to trust in the choices we make.

I Carry a Lot

Jacqueline Knight

Well, I carry a lot and it's been a long time. I'm still carrying it. My children are grown. They feel they can tell me what to do and it's alright. I worry about other people's feelings. How they feel and what they think and what they say.

Being on my own has been a big problem for me because I am very nice, etc. I talk to people, listen to what they say, do things when they ask.

This is what I carry.

I just want to sit here and think about how much I carry without considering myself.

BAG LADY

Kameka Goodwin

I am known as the bag lady. I carry a lot. Maybe I carry too much. If I don't carry it, who will?

Day in and day out my bags are with me. I have the baggage from a rough childhood. I carry bags from the broken promises of past relationships. When I awake, I immediately pick up the bag and hold on to it while trying to make it through another day without having an emotional breakdown because he's gone.

I carry the baggage of taking care of a family who is trying to put the pieces of its life back together. I head to work with my lunch bag, my computer bag, my school bag and the baggage of being a low-income individual looking to one day be debt free.

The bag that was handed to me from my culture seems unbearable at times. The bag that houses leadership for my children is a permanent bag that I drag everywhere I go.

I can't freely move and soar because of my bags, but I feel that I need them. I have had them with me so long, I don't know what to do with them. If I could only sit them down and walk away from them. I don't know what I would do if I was bag free. I would love to experience a day of no bags.

I've been told that I need to check my bags and get on my plane and fly to higher grounds.

Monique Blodgett

Who do you think you are

No

Do you know who I am

no

I don't think you truly know

Who I am

What I carry Inside of me

Yes I am a woman

Yes I can bear children

Yes I am black

Yes I am emotional at times

And yes my voice can touch heaven,

And be heard down in hell

But that don't equal

An Angry Black Woman

You see

There is something more vicious

More vile

More scarier out there, that not even

The devil is ready to go to war with

And it walks among you

Every single day and every single night

Do you hear it?

Can you see it?

Do you feel it?

Do you feel this power?

This power that strikes up and down my spine

Fuels my body

And transforms my eyes

As my stare decapitates your presence

my tongue is set on fire

and my soul screams out

Don't you touch my child

Don't you look at her with lustful eyes

Don't you even try to think that

You

Will take her away from me

With your tricks, laws and subconscious hints

Of self-destruction and mind control bullshit

She is my seed

And She came from ME

So go take it up with God

If you don't want to believe me

I will fight you with all of my heart

With all of my might

Every bit of my mind

And a prayer to God before I arrive (unleash)

For I am awakened

I am the beast

when it comes to protecting what came from me

I am loving and Nurturing

and I can smile with dignity

but I am Not just some soulless monster

that blindly destroys everything

For I am the provider,

Professor and protector of my seed

I hold 1000's of years of my ancestors' knowledge and experiences that have

Prepared me to protect my child and any other child who is in need

and I live

To love

To fight

To breathe

To see Life

for as long as it is meant to be

And I will protect

Against anyone and anything

Who comes for me

And my seed

THE BEAST

This poem is dedicated to Korryn Gaines who lost her life

while protecting her son.

Inspired by the artwork of Autumn Gavrielle Armstrong

titled "Self Defense is Self Love"

Greater Than Me (Feeling Inferior)

Vicki Alexander

I am self-conscious when I am with my sisters and
brothers who have not had as much privilege as I have. I
am self conscious about my light skin in a black reality. I
am self-conscious of having privilege that comes along
with being a doctor in this country. I am even self-
conscious of having privilege because I have retirement
funds to maintain a comfortable modest life style at the
age of 75.

I have had the experience of raising a child from birth but
not being pregnant and giving birth. Yet, for more than
twenty years, I delivered hundreds of other women's
babies. For many years, I had the opportunity to
collectively study the origins of women's oppression and
oppression of black folks in America. It is one thing to
actually carry and reproduce a child by giving birth and
completely another thing to nurture and raise a child. At
nearly every birth I have felt self-conscious that I never

experienced the pain of actually delivering, nor have I felt the ecstasy, sense of accomplishment and release when the baby is pushed out of the birth canal.

Wait a minute. Why should I feel this self-conscious guilt? Why should I feel inferior? I have been able to overcome many obstacles and am proud. But, the guilt is deep. I did nothing wrong. This is not guilt. It is being self-conscious. It is important to recognize the privilege that has allowed me to get to where I am. Why hasn't every child had the opportunity that came my way to develop their mind, their skills and their leadership capability? This makes me angry.

What I carry is a deep self-consciousness that I have had privilege of a strong family background. I have been called Mulatto, Negro, Black, African American, and black American. History clearly defines me as a conscious member of the African American community. Blackness is not based on shades of a color. My state of consciousness as I walk down the street is that of a Black person in America. My state of consciousness is a deep intellectual, experiential and emotional feeling of connectedness. I feel connected to the history, struggles, and victories of our people. I cherish and continuously develop that deep sense of connectedness and will continue to fight in the struggle for freedom, justice, equality and equity in all things. I am feeling emotionally emancipated. Nothing can stop me. This is my life.

Discussion Questions

- How do these stories illustrate the resilience and strength of the author(s)?
- How have the stories in this book impacted you?
- How do stories help us learn about the world?
- Write a letter to a local lawmaker in which you tell that person your concerns about a situation that comes up in these stories with your recommendations of what needs to be done to improve this situation to give those impacted opportunities to thrive. What are your concerns?
- Based on these stories, what do the health care, childcare and education systems currently look like for you and your family? What should they look like?

Healthy Black Families, Inc. Programs and Services

Sisters Together Empowering Peers (S.T.E.P.) Program

S.T.E.P. began in 2002 and is a peer-led support and empowerment group that addresses health and social inequities for African American parenting women in our community. Many STEP women start their journey through the Black Infant Health Program, (BIHP), who we partner with and provide support. STEP Leadership provides continued education on issues such as access to essential goods and services, i.e., housing, education, job training, school readiness, and health information. Our "kitchen table" talks provide opportunities to share information and experiences. Please join our Sisters' Circle! We meet every 4th Thursday, 6-8PM at The Rec. Room, 3222 Adeline Street, in Berkeley Childcare, food and support is provided…

Community Health Prep and Leadership Training

The Community Health Worker Preparation training is a fun, interactive and co-learning experience. It builds upon the strengths, skills and leadership capacities of our program participants who are interested in advocating for and providing peer support, networking, information and resources to African American parents and their families. Our health education and prevention topics include breastfeeding, nutrition, prenatal/postpartum health, stress management, health equity and career development. To empower our families to become leaders and advocates to take action in bringing positive change in their community, we provide topics in leadership, problem solving, navigating complicated systems, community organizing and outreach, and social, economic and environmental justice. The training is funded by the San Francisco Foundation. The training also better prepares participants to pursue a Community Health Worker Certificate from an accredited college while encouraging positive social change.

Thirsty For Change! Program

HBF Inc., in partnership with the Center for Food, Faith and Justice is working to create an atmosphere of healthy eating and drinking for our families and community and to foster a cultural change that supports the elimination of health inequities created by the predatory proliferation of soda and junk food in our communities.

"Thirsty for Change!" is engaging African Americans in South and West Berkeley through providing a broad array of fun and creative activities for parents, their children and families to improve health through nutritious foods, cooking, community gardening and art. Our approach includes listening to our community's needs and ideas, creating youth water ambassadors, conducting workshops on "Soil to Soul gardening," engaging in art, poetry and artistic activities for community education. We sustain ourselves through publishing our evaluation findings for community and civic leaders to encourage continuous healthy behavior and policy change to improve our health.

What I Carry

Notes Pages

*

Made in the USA
Las Vegas, NV
23 June 2021